DAD JOKES

THE LAUGH-OUT-LOUD EDITION

hamlyn

First published in Great Britain in 2023 by Hamlyn, an imprint of Octopus Publishing Group Ltd
Carmelite House
50 Victoria Embankment
London EC4Y 0DZ
www.octopusbooks.co.uk

An Hachette UK Company
www.hachette.co.uk

Text Copyright © Kit Chilvers 2023
Design and layout copyright © Octopus Publishing Group Ltd 2023

Distributed in the US by Hachette Book Group
1290 Avenue of the Americas
4th and 5th Floors, New York, NY 10104

Distributed in Canada by Canadian Manda Group
664 Annette St., Toronto, Ontario, Canada M6S 2C8

Kit Chilvers asserts the moral right to be identified as the author of this work.

ISBN 978 1 78325 546 7

A CIP catalogue record for this book is available from the British Library.

Printed and bound in the UK

10 9 8 7 6 5 4 3 2 1

Publisher: Stephanie Jackson
Senior Editor: Pauline Bache
Junior Editor: Louisa Johnson
Editorial Assistant: Constance Lam
Designer: The Oak Studio
Art Director: Jaz Bahra
Senior Production Manager: Katherine Hockley

This FSC® label means that materials used for this product have been responsibly sourced.

MIX
Paper from responsible sources
FSC® C104740

DAD JOKES

THE LAUGH-OUT-LOUD EDITION

@DadSaysJokes

hamlyn

Dedicated to Shena:
wife, mother and the source
of so many wife jokes.

Introduction

And here we are again... another volume of dad jokes.

From knee-slappers to puns that will make your whole family groan, this fantastic volume has it all – a dad joke for every occasion.

Here at @DadSaysJokes, we're also building our humour network on different video platforms, such as TikTok and YouTube. So hopefully a new audience of people will be able to love, laugh at and loathe our new gamified dad joke-athons.

Thanks to our dedicated band of japesters, as always. Please keep the comments coming on Twitter, Instagram and Facebook. We really couldn't do this without you – and the world is no fun if there are no jokers.

What did the Lego set say to the king?

We come in pieces.

———

What can leap higher than a tall building?

Anything. Tall buildings can't leap.

If you do your writing on an Apple device, you end up writing MacBook Prose.

———

What do you call a chickpea that walks off a cliff?

Fala-fell.

I had a terrible nightmare in which I was forced to eat my own clone.

I almost pooped myself.

———————

I took my dog to the lake today and noticed he floats really well.

He's a very good buoy.

Me: When we go to marriage counselling later, you're going to bring up my obsession with predicting the future, aren't you?

My wife: Yes.

Me: I *knew* it!

What do you call a doctor who is always on call?

An on-call-ogist.

_____

I received a flyer on anger management the other day.

I lost it.

All the toilets in the police station have been stolen.

Detectives have nothing to go on.

I'm opening a new gym, and the instructors are going to go from door to door around the neighbourhood, telling people about the benefits of joining it.

I've named it Jehovah's Fitness.

———————

For the past 25 years, I've received a Valentine's card from a secret admirer. I was upset I didn't get one this year.

First my gran dies, now this!

What does the tiniest vampire in the world get up to at night?

Your ankles.

_____

Three tons of hair have been stolen from a wig factory.

Police are combing the area.

I attended a noisy legal hearing, and the judge started yelling, "Order! Order!"

So I said, "A pastrami on rye, please."

_____

My wife says that I wasted money by ordering a giant frame for our wedding photo.

Well, I think she should look at the bigger picture.

I saw a bunch of ants eating my chocolate bar on the kitchen counter.

This means there is life on Mars.

———————

Did you hear about the sale on paddles?

It was quite the oar-deal.

I bet *nobody* will see this one coming.

1.

I recently bought a new toilet brush.

Long story short, I'm going back to paper.

———

A friend of mine tries to impress girls by drawing realistic pictures of the Ford F-150.

He's a pick-up artist.

Why did the grape cross the road?

No raisin.

———

Why didn't the melons get married?

Because they cantaloupe.

Wealthy Frenchman: Let me show you my yachts. This is *Un*, this is *Deux*, this is *Trois*, this is *Quatre*, this is *Six*.

Me: Where's the fifth one?

Wealthy Frenchman: *Cinq*.

How do you stop a dog from barking in the back of a car?

Put him in the front.

My partner has banned me from making breakfast puns.

They say if I make any more, I'm toast.

But my kids keep egging me on.

———————

Did you hear about the antiques collector who found an old Coca-Cola lamp?

She was soda lighted.

What does Pac-Man put on his tacos?

Guaca-waka-waka-mole.

———

My wife is a bodybuilder.

She's pregnant.

There are three unwritten rules of life...

1.

2.

3.

What has two butts and kills people?

An assassin.

What do you call fake potatoes?

Imitaters.

Siri kept calling me Shirley today.

I was starting to get really angry and then I realized why.

I'd left my phone on *Airplane* mode.

———————

In "laughter", the "L" comes first...

... and the rest of the letters come aughter.

My wife just confessed that she broke my favourite lamp.

I don't think I'll be able to look at her in the same light ever again.

My friend couldn't afford his water bill.

So I sent him a "Get Well Soon" card.

Spring is here!

I got so excited I wet my plants!

My battery died the other day.

It was AA tragedy.

_____

Bilbo awoke one morning to find that a supermarket had been built next to his house.

There was an unexpected item in the Baggins area.

Where can you buy and sell used shrimp?

The prawn shop.

————————

Where did Vader get his degree?

Darthmouth College.

What do you call it when a cat wins first place at a dog show?

A cat-has-trophy!

———————

I'm writing a movie about broken bones.

I just need a cast for it.

What do you call a cow with no legs?

Ground beef.

My husband and I sometimes disagree about whether to add eggs to cream.

Custardy disputes are always rough.

———————

Why are fish so smart?

Because they live in schools.

Me: Doctor, every time I drink coffee, I get a pain in my eye.

Doctor: Try taking the spoon out of your cup.

What is a small pigeon called?

A smidgen.

———————

Last night, my wife and I watched a couple of DVDs back to back.

Luckily, I was the one facing the TV.

I went to see an archaeologist at a comedy bar.

All he did was dig up old jokes.

_____

What do you call a book on voyeurism?

A Peeping Tome.

How do you get down from an elephant?

You don't get down from an elephant. You get down from a goose.

My last job was mowing the cemetery.
It was a pretty important role.

I worked above hundreds of people.

———————

Why don't space rocks have pants on?

Because they forgot their asteroid belt.

Me: I'm nervous about meeting your dad. How can I impress him?

My girlfriend: He's really into cars.

Me: OK.

Later...

Her dad: Hi, nice to meet you.

Me: Right – let's talk about Pixar's finest movie.

I told the carpet fitter not to carpet my steps.

He gave me a blank stair.

———

I hate my job. All I do is crush cans all day.

It's just soda pressing.

The doctor handed me a cup and said: "Urinate."

"Thanks," I said. "I thought I was a six out of ten at best."

_____

I got home from work this evening to find my kids have been on eBay all day.

If they're still there tomorrow, I'll lower the price.

My partner says I get bad tempered when I drink whiskey, so I switched to Canadian whiskey.

I'm still bad tempered, but now I'm sorry, too.

———————

My favourite dishes are all cooked with petroleum by-products.

I guess you could say I have refined taste.

My dog accidentally swallowed a whole bag of Scrabble tiles. We took him to the vet to get him checked out.

No word yet.

What do you call a woman who tells dad jokes?

A faux pa.

Not everyone thinks Cleopatra is beautiful.

But that's how Julius Caesar.

My local Renaissance festival is holding auditions for knights tomorrow at 4pm.

Be there or be squire.

How do you buy a discounted boat?

You look for sails.

I asked a librarian if she had a book about Pavlov's dogs and Schrödinger's cat.

She said it rang a bell, but she wasn't sure if it was there or not.

———————

I love bad puns.

It's just how eye roll.

I hurt my knee slipping on ice in front of the police station.

I went inside to complain, but they charged me with a felony.

———

My friend got a job repairing ladders.

He's working his way to the top.

Apparently, keeping tropical fish at home can have a calming effect on the brain.

Must be all the indoor fins.

My partner said I have to stop making puns of the names of world capitals.

You win some, Jerusalem.

———————

Killing your father is called patricide.

Killing your mother is called matricide.

So, what is killing your friend called?

Homie-cide.

Socrates: To do is to be.

Plato: To be is to do.

Scooby: Do be do.

What crime-fighting duo hangs out at the noodle shop?

Batman and Ramen.

———————

You know, a lot of people say they pick their nose, but I feel like I was just born with mine.

What kind of pizza did the pilot prefer?

Plane.

———————

A man loses three fingers in a work accident.

He asks the doctor, "Can I drive with this hand?"

The doctor replies, "Maybe. But I wouldn't count on it."

What did one colour
say to the
other colour?

I love hue.

Neighbour: Hey, can I borrow your stepladder?

Me: Sure! Here, it's in my garage.

Neighbour: That's just a regular ladder.

Me: No, it's a stepladder. My wife brought it from her previous marriage.

How do trees access the internet?

They log in.

Why did the chicken go to the gym?

To work on his pecks.

You're living, you occupy space and you have mass.

You know what that means?

You matter.

_____

I just can't stop listening to 1970s rock bands.

I may be developing OC/DC.

What do you call a pony with a sore throat?

A little horse.

_____

A physicist and a biologist went on a date...

... but there was no chemistry.

Me: What do you know about atoms?

Son: Very little.

Me: Besides that.

Did you hear that the inventor of autocorrect died?

May he rust in pieces.

I was having some abdominal pain, so I went to the library to get a medical book to help me diagnose what was wrong.

Annoyingly, somebody had ripped out the appendix.

There is a new trend in our office; everyone is naming their food.

I noticed it today, while I was eating a sandwich named Kevin.

I just couldn't bring myself to quit my job at the bakery.

I was underpaid and the hours were lousy, but I needed the bread.

Having too much sex can cause memory loss.

I know, because I read it on page 87 in a medical journal on 14 November 2019 at 3.19pm.

Why don't vultures pay excess baggage fees?

They only fly with carrion.

———————

What's the difference between a simple person and a pizza?

One is easy to cheat, the other is cheesy to eat.

I used to have a job cutting holes to make trapdoors for theatres.

It was just a stage I was going through.

_____

Did you hear about the cat that ate a ball of yarn?

She had mittens.

Did you hear they arrested the devil?

They got him on possession.

Did you hear about the surgeon who enjoyed performing quick operations on insects?

He did one on the fly.

_____

I have a friend who worships certain shades of blue.

He's a cyan-tologist.

Where do spiders seek health advice?

WebMD.

_____

I use rectal thermometers because I was told they are more accurate.

But they sure taste worse!

This morning,
I coughed up a
pawn, a knight and
a bishop.

I must have a
chess infection.

My cat has just eaten three mallards.

He's a duck-filled fatty puss.

———

What's the quickest way to double your money?

Hold it in front of a mirror.

Oxygen and magnesium went on a date.

Everyone was like, "OMg!"

—————

Where are mathematicians buried?

The symmetry.

Did you hear about the pregnant
bed bug?

She'll be having a baby in the spring.

_____

What do you call Santa without GPS?

A lost Claus.

Why couldn't the jalapeño do archery?

He didn't habanero.

———

I'm regretting becoming vegetarian.

It was a huge missed steak.

I insulted my friend Terry in public, and I feel awful.

I must be suffering from dissin' terry.

———

What did the volcano say to his partner?

I lava you.

What does the chromosome like to wear at the weekend?

Genes.

———————

I put up a high-voltage electric fence around my property over the weekend.

My neighbour is dead against it.

I let a pasta chef borrow my car.

He returned it all denty.

Why did the iPhone go to the dentist?

He had a blue tooth.

———

Why don't dolphins have legs?

It would de-feet the whole porpoise.

Student: I'm reading a new book in school.

Me: Oh yeah, what's it called?

Student: *Animal Farm*.

Me: Orwell?

Student: Yes, it's going great, thanks!

I was driving to the airport to catch my flight when I saw a sign that said "Airport left".

So I turned around and went home.

———————

I'm throwing a space-themed party for my birthday.

But I don't want to planet.

I've just finished writing a book
on snakes.

It would have been much easier if
I'd just written it on paper...

_____

What kind of sticks do bouncers use?

Pogo sticks.

What do you call a detective who solves cases accidentally?

Sheer Luck Holmes.

_____

I've been banned from the Secret Cooking Society...

I kept spilling the beans.

My 12-year-old son tried coffee for the first time today.

He told me that it tasted like dirt.

I told him it was just ground this morning.

A witch was flying along on her broom when she noticed that all the other witches were flying on vacuum cleaners.

She thought, "Am I the only one still driving a stick?"

———————

When I was in college, I was rejected from every fraternity because I was circumcised.

Apparently, you need to be a complete dick.

people ask me
why i only type
dad jokes using
lowercase letters.

the truth is, i
stopped giving
a shift a long
time ago.

The best gift I ever received was a broken drum.

You can't beat that.

_____

I want to create a product that's a laxative, but also contains painkillers for the burn.

I'll call it "Ibepoopin".

Do you know how scientists freshen their breath?

With experi-mints.

———

Why do plants hate maths?

It gives them square roots.

I recently saw a sign that said
"Watch for animals".

What a great deal!

_____

I'm an expert at picking leaves and
heating them in water.

It's my special tea.

What did one wall say to the other wall?

"I'll meet you at the corner."

I don't suffer from insanity.

I enjoy every minute of it.

———————

I took a job as an executioner, but it's been tough.

I'm really struggling to get ahead.

Did you hear about the man going around painting people's houses illegally?

They caught him red-handed.

_____

I've just had some terrible news: my barber says he can't cut my hair any longer.

Apparently he can only cut it shorter.

Can anyone tell me what "IDK" means?

Every time I ask someone, they say,
"I don't know."

———

My boss says he is going to fire the
employee with the worst posture.

I have a hunch it's going to be me.

My kids refused to eat leftover tacos for dinner, so my partner asked me to throw them out.

I did.

But now I have no idea what to do with the tacos.

What would two termites order at a restaurant?

Table for two.

———

My partner threatened to leave me because of my "filthy and disgusting habits".

I was so shocked I nearly choked on my toenails.

How many nuns does it take to change a lightbulb?

Nun!

_____

When the ex-president's treason trial ended with a death by hanging sentence, what did he really begin to pray for?

Fake noose!

I had a quiet game of tennis today.

It's just like regular tennis, but without the racket.

———

I work for the Forest Service, and my boss told me to mark the trails with cairns.

He said, "Leave no turn unstoned."

Look, it's not working out between us. For starters, I'm sick of your terrible jokes.

I understand. And for the main course?

Why did Noah have so much difficulty fishing on the Ark?

He only brought two worms.

———————

I am getting a little sick of my wife complaining that I sit around and do nothing all weekend.

I'm not going to stand for it.

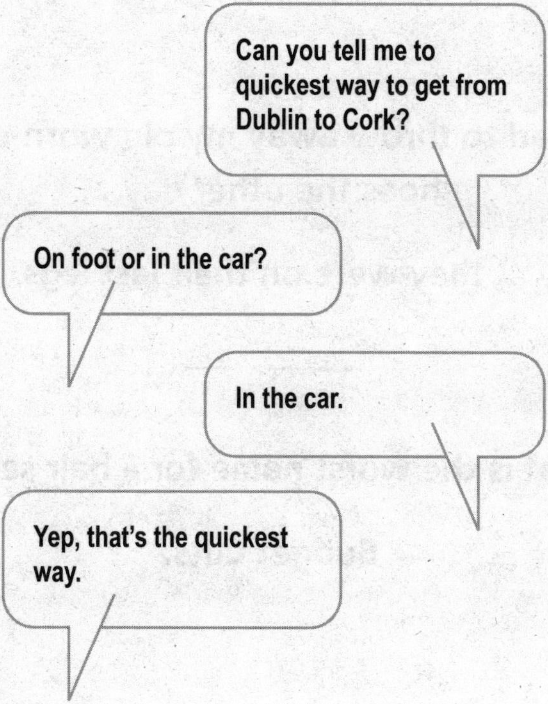
Can you tell me to quickest way to get from Dublin to Cork?
On foot or in the car?
In the car.
Yep, that's the quickest way.

I had to throw away my old worn-out shoes the other day…

… they were on their last legs.

———

What is the worst name for a hair salon?

Budget Cuts.

Can anyone tell me what oblivious means?

I have no idea.

———

I've opened a restaurant called "Peace and Quiet".

Kids' meals only $150.

What happens when the devil goes bald?

There'll be hell toupée.

———

How do you feed 100 people with one loaf of bread?

Cut off the ends. Now you have endless bread.

What kind of streets do ghosts haunt?

Dead ends.

––––––––––

I had a date tonight. It was perfect.

Tomorrow, I'll try a grape.

What do you call a cow in an earthquake?

A milkshake.

What do you call a zombie who doesn't joke around?

Dead serious.

———————

If at first you don't succeed...

... skydiving is not for you.

I swallowed two strings. When I passed them, they were tied.

I kid you knot.

_____

How many lawyers does it take to change a lightbulb?

One to climb the ladder, one to shake it and one to sue the ladder company.

During dinner, I told my wife,
"I used to be grapes."

She said, "Huh?"

I replied, "Sorry. It must be the
wine talking."

———————

My partner begged me not to tell
anyone about their foot fetish.

Well, I've only gone and put my foot
in it.

The inventor of the crossword puzzle moved into my neighbourhood.

He lives five streets down and two houses across.

_____

What do you call a pig that does karate?

A pork chop.

A pun, a play on words and a limerick walk into a bar.

No joke.

I taught my kids about democracy tonight by casting a vote on what movie to watch and what pizza to order.

Then I picked the movie and pizza I wanted, because they're not of voting age.

———————

I'm gonna quit the rat race and become a sculptor.

One of my mates did it, and he's already made six figures!

What do you get when you cross a cocker spaniel and a hairstylist's poodle?

A cocker poodle doo!

Why did the tomato turn red?

Because it saw the salad dressing.

You just got turned into a ghost. Where is the first place you go for help?

The ICU.

_____

IKEA had to cancel their new artificial intelligence programme.

In less than a week, the system became shelf-aware.

What's the difference between
my wallet before children and
after children?

Now, there are pictures where the
money used to be.

———————

I haven't spoken to my brother-in-law
in four years.

I thought it would be rude to
interrupt him!

I'm at the airport and there's a woman passed out on the baggage carousel.

She's slowly coming around.

Just found out that "Aaaaaaarrrrrggggghhhhh" isn't a real word.

I can't tell you how angry I am!

———————

Some people shave their heads for charity, but instead, I decided to comb my hair in two different directions.

I'm just trying to do my part.

What do you call a biography made entirely out of memes?

A meme-oir.

If I were to ask someone to marry me, I'd propose in an elevator.

That way, I could quickly take our relationship to the next level.

I told my wife that a husband is like a fine wine: we just get better with age.

The next day, she locked me in the cellar.

———————

My boss calls me "the computer".

It's nothing to do with intelligence; I just go to sleep if left unattended for 15 minutes.

What vegetable
should you never
bring on a boat?

A leek.

Doctor: So, you're telling me that you have a problem with one of your ears. Are you sure?

Me: Yes, doctor. I am definite.

What do you call a man who has a car above his head?

Jack.

———————

Just got a call from my son's school. The principal told me that he's been acting up in class.

I said, "He acts up at home all the time, but I don't call you, do I?"

Why do Italian policemen always carry bread around with them?

Foccacia'n criminals.

What do you call a lady who carries people across rivers?

Bridget.

People are usually shocked that I have a police record.

But I love their greatest hits.

_____

Never share a secret with a clock.

Time will tell.

What's a vampire's favourite ship?

A blood vessel.

———————

I'm afraid for my calendar.

Its days are numbered.

Why do bulls make terrible salesmen?

They charge too much.

———

Singing in the shower is fun until you get bubbles in your mouth.

Then it's a soap opera.

Dear maths,

Grow up and solve your own problems.

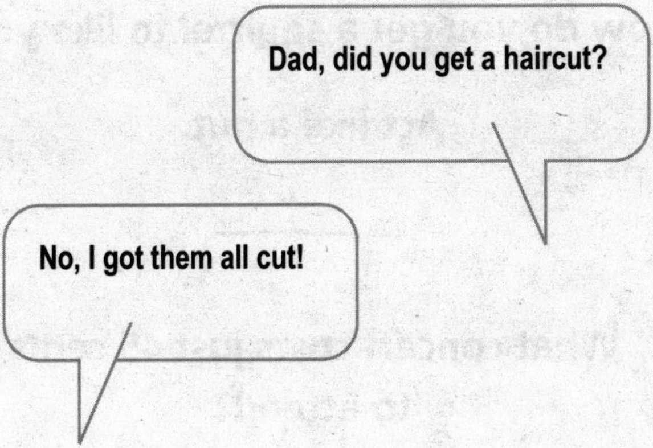
Dad, did you get a haircut?
No, I got them all cut!

How do you get a squirrel to like you?

Act like a nut.

_____

What concert costs just 45 cents
to attend?

50 Cent featuring Nickelback.

If a child refuses to nap, are they guilty of resisting a rest?

_____

I used to play piano by ear.

Now I use my hands. It works much better.

Why can't you hear
a psychiatrist using
the bathroom?

Because the "P"
is silent.

Did you hear about the circus fire?

It was in tents.

———

What unit do you use to measure the mass of an influencer's following?

Instagrams!

"Queue" is spelled "Q" followed by four silent letters.

No, it's just "Q". The other letters are just waiting their turn.

A Buddhist monk approaches a hotdog stand and says, "Make me one with everything."

How easy is it to count in binary?

It's as easy as 01, 10, 11.

There's a fine line between a denominator and a numerator.

Only a fraction of you will understand this.

———

Have you heard about the Disney virus?

It makes everything on your computer go Goofy.

Dear algebra, stop asking us to find your X.

She's never coming back.

Have you heard about corduroy pillows?

They're making headlines.

———————

I bought the world's worst thesaurus yesterday.

Not only is it terrible, it's also terrible!

If you get pregnant in the Amazon, it's next-day delivery.

I spent the weekend building a time machine, so that's 48 hours of my life that I'm definitely getting back.

I attempted to combine nitrous oxide and broth, but all it did was make me a laughing stock.

I used to live hand to mouth. Do you know what changed my life?

Cutlery.

———————

My son has suggested that I register for a donor card.

He's a man after my own heart.

I needed an eight-character-long password so I picked Snow White and the Seven Dwarfs.

I've just been on a once-in-a-lifetime holiday.

I'll tell you what – never again.

Getting a drive-thru McDonald's was more expensive than I thought.

Once you've hired the car...

As a child, I was made to walk the plank.

We couldn't afford a dog.

How do moths swim?

Using the butterfly stroke.

_____

Two flies are playing football in a saucer.

One says to the other, "Make an effort, mate. We're playing in the cup tomorrow."

I bought some Armageddon cheese today. The packet said "Best Before End".

———————

Our son has a great deal of willpower – and even more won't power.

Did you hear the one about the kid who started a business tying shoelaces on the playground?

It was a knot-for-profit.

Sore throats are a real pain in the neck.

I gave my children some birth control advice.

Contraceptives should be used on every conceivable occasion.

**Before the invention of the wheel...
everything was a drag!**

_____

Why don't crabs donate to charity?

Because they're shellfish.

A man went to a fortune teller and said, "I want my palms read."

So she hit his hands with a hammer.

_____

I wouldn't say I'm a bad cook...

... but I do use the smoke alarm as a timer.

I took someone else's drink at the café yesterday, but I couldn't finish it.

It just wasn't my cup of tea.

What did the fish say when he swam into a wall?

"Damn!"

_____

Did you hear what happened when the guy who wrote "The Hokey Pokey" died?

They couldn't close his coffin.

Every time they put his right foot in, he put his left foot out.

What sits at the bottom of the sea and twitches?

A nervous wreck.

_____

How does Moses make his tea?

He brews it.

Why should the number 288 never be mentioned?

It's two gross.

_____

What did the buffalo say when his son left for college?

"Bison."

Why did the yogurt go to the opera?

Because it was cultured.

————————

How do English teachers say hello?

"Hey, haven't we metaphor?"

Why did the custard cream go to the dentist?

Because he lost his filling.

Why is it annoying to eat next to basketball players?

They dribble all the time.

———————

How many times can you subtract 10 from 100?

Once.

The next time, you would be subtracting 10 from 90.

Why do bees have sticky hair?

Because they use honeycombs.

———————

Why did it get so hot in the basketball stadium after the game?

All the fans left.

Why can't male ants sink?

They're buoy-ant.

If four out of five people suffer
from diarrhoea…

… does that mean that one enjoys it?

_____

Why did the gym close down?

Because it never worked out.

What type of sandals do frogs wear?

Open-toad sandals.

Why doesn't the sun need to go to university?

Because it has a million degrees!

———————

Why is the UK the wettest country?

Because the king is always reigning.

What are a shark's favourite words?

"Man overboard!"

Did you hear about the Italian chef who died?

He pasta-way.

Why does Snoop Dogg use an umbrella?

For drizzle.

_____

What kind of tea is hard to swallow?

Reality.

My New Year's resolution is to procrastinate.

I'll start tomorrow.

What's the most terrifying word in nuclear physics?

"Oops!"

_____

My pregnant wife asked me if I was worried her body temperature is too hot for the baby inside her.

I said, "Nope. It's womb temperature."

Grasshopper: Hi there. I'll have a beer.

Bartender: Did you know we have a cocktail named after you?

Grasshopper: Wait, you have a cocktail called Dave?

My husband said he's leaving me because of my obsession with supermarkets.

I said to him, "I understand. Would you like any assistance packing?"

What nationality is Santa?

North Polish.

Some trees are committed to one romantic relationship at a time.

They practise mahogany.

———

I have a clean conscience.

It's never been used.

How do you deal with a fear of speed bumps?

You slowly get over it.

I wish my grey hair started in Las Vegas...

... because what happens in Vegas, stays in Vegas.

How does a lawyer say goodbye?

"I'll be suing ya!"

———

Why don't atheists solve exponential equations?

They don't believe in higher powers.

I have to make bad chemistry jokes...

... because all the good ones argon.

———————

Why do lazy people eat toilet paper?

So it wipes on the way out.

What do you call a vegetable that has escaped prison?

An esca-pea.

_____

What are goosebumps for?

To stop geese speeding.

Why did the team of witches always lose their cricket matches?

Their bats kept flying away.

Why didn't the leopard enjoy playing hide and seek?

Because he was spotted all the time.

———————

How do you count cows?

With a cow-culator.

Where do mice park their boats?

At the hickory dickory dock.

———————

Why do grizzly bears have hairy coats?

Fur protection.

How do you tell a baby snake from an adult snake?

The baby snake has a rattle.

———————

What is the least interesting beast in the entire animal kingdom?

The boar.

Why did all the rabbits go on strike?

They wanted a better celery.

I have never hunted bear...

... but I once went fishing in just
my shorts.

I can't stand jokes about insects.

They really bug me.

My daughter wanted to dress up as a rodent control worker for Halloween.

I said, "Sure, gopher it."

_____

Imagine how excited barn owls were when people invented barns.

Me: One packet of birdseed, please.

Cashier: Here you go. That's £2.50.

Me: Thanks. How long does it take for the birds to grow once I plant them?

Why are cats the best salesmen?

They are very purr-suasive.

———

What did the beaver say to the tree?

Nice gnawing you.

My friend just broke the world record for getting the largest number of pigeons to land on him.

The guy's a ledge.

What does a female snake use for support?

A co-bra.

I went for a job at the local stables. They asked me if I had ever shoed a horse before.

I said, "No, but I once said boo to a donkey."

Me: Does your horse smoke?

Farmer: No.

Me: Well in that case, I think your stable is on fire.

I can always tell if someone is lying just by looking at them.

I can also tell if they are standing.

———————

A Spanish magician announced he would disappear on the count of three.

He began: *"Uno… dos…"*

And then he disappeared without a *tres*.

A locksmith had to go to court to give evidence last week.

Apparently, he was the key witness.

Why don't skeletons ever go trick
or treating?

Because they have no body to go with.

What do you call cheese that
isn't yours?

Nacho cheese.

Shout out to the all people asking what the opposite of "in" is.

I bought a brand new hearse.

I'm dying to get into it!

I thought about going on an almond-only diet.

But that's just nuts.

———

I used to work in a shoe recycling shop.

It was sole destroying.

Did I tell you about the time I fell in love during a backflip?

I was heels over head.

———

People don't like having to bend down to get their drinks.

We really need to raise the bar.

Dad: Can you put the cat out?

Son: I didn't know it was on fire.

I was a doctor for a while, but then I quit.

I just didn't have enough patience.

_____

I recently found out that there is no training for garbage men.

They just pick things up as they go along.

How do dumpsters communicate with each other?

They trash talk.

I purchased a new car at the dealership. Unfortunately for me, the reverse gear doesn't work.

There's no going back now.

At the age of 92, my grandma started walking six miles every day.

She is now 95, and we have no idea where she is.

The way my family is structured is extremely toxic.

It's a nuclear family.

———————

My son just started eating $100 bills.

I guess he has very expensive taste.

Pride is what you feel when your kids net $150 from your yard sale.

Panic is what you feel when you realize your car is missing!

———————

I just purchased a book on obsession.

I read it 20 times.

The man who invented cough drops has died.

Apparently, there will be no coffin at his funeral.

People say that love is the best feeling, but I think that finding a toilet when you have diarrhoea is better.

_____

If you think nobody cares if you're alive, try missing a couple of payments.

The shinbone is a device used for locating furniture in a dark room.

I almost dropped my phone on my soft carpeted floor, but thankfully I have lightning-fast reflexes, and was able to slap it into the concrete wall instead.

If you ever see me out jogging, please kill whatever is chasing me.

_____

Dear Santa,

I would like a new birthday suit this year.

My current one is old, wrinkled and sagging.

When I was a kid, I literally thought that "This little piggy went to market" meant it went shopping.

I'll never tell my accountant a joke again.

He just depreciates them.

A man and a giraffe walk into a bar.

After a few drinks, the giraffe falls over and dies. The man begins to walk out, but the bartender stops him.

"Hey, you can't leave that lyin' there!" the bartender yells.

The man turns around and says, "It's not a lion. It's a giraffe."

———————

I am always late for work, but I make up for it by always leaving early.

I took an exam last week to see if I could become an insect inspector.

I think I will get the job, because I boxed all the right ticks.

I worked for a few months as a tailor last year, but I decided to quit.

I wasn't really suited for it, and the work was sew-sew.

If you need a job, you could always try search and rescue.

They're always looking for people.

Why did the man have to quit his job fixing baths, sinks and showers?

The work was just too draining.

———————

I got a commerce degree and then tried my luck as an investment banker.

It was a fun gig for a while, but I eventually quit because I lost interest.

Son: Dad, I have something to tell you. I have an imaginary girlfriend.

Dad: You know, you could do a lot better.

Son: Thanks, Dad. That means a lot.

Dad: Not you. I was talking to your girlfriend.

I have a hilarious joke about a courier...

... but I'm afraid you may not get it.

_____

How can you tell if a lead singer is at your front door?

He is not sure where to come in and he is unable to find the key.

In retail, there are two important things to learn: honesty and empathy.

The sooner you learn to fake these, the better you will be at your job.

———————

Where do typists go to get drunk?

The space bar.

I had a job selling bras for a while, but I couldn't support myself.

_____

I've been trying to break up with an optician recently. It's really hard!

Every time I tell her I can't see her anymore, she moves an inch closer and says, "How about now?"

What do you call a man in shark-infested waters?

Chum.

_____

What do you get when a turkey lays an egg on top of a barn?

An egg roll.

Mom is mad at me.
She asked me to
sync her phone...

... so I threw it in
the ocean.

The man who invented the word search has just died. His funeral will be held next...

```
T U I S B V G M M P

H J G U O N Q U X

N M A N T A Q W Z

B T U E S D A Y P G

H C V N K O T D I M
```

I was going to go on an expensive vacation with a classical pianist, but she was too baroque.

I can tolerate algebra, maybe even a little calculus...

... but geometry is where I draw the line.

I was just at the shop and realized I can't afford to buy any pasta.

I'm penne-less.

———————

I was walking on the beach when I saw a shark circling a swimmer. The swimmer was yelling for help.

I just laughed. I knew that shark wasn't going to help him.

What do you call a man who is always stealing stuff?

Rob.

_____

What do knights put on their pancakes?

Sir Up.

Where do hamburgers go dancing?

A meat-ball!

When a toddler reaches the "why?" stage, it's like opening a bottle of champagne.

Once it's uncorked, there's no going back.

What happened when the Easter Bunny met the rabbit of his dreams?

They lived hoppily ever after.

———————

What do you get when you combine a Christmas tree with a computer?

A pine-apple.

What is the difference between a cat that got photocopied and a cat that follows you?

One is a cat copy; the other is a copycat.

Why don't pirates shower before they walk the plank?

Because they'll just wash up on shore later.

———————

Why was the fraction nervous about marrying the decimal?

Because he would have to convert.

What's the one thing you are guaranteed to get every year on your birthday?

Older.

_____

Two pickles fell out of a jar on to the floor. What did one say to the other?

"Dill with it."

How many chocolate bunnies can you put into an empty Easter basket?

Only one, because after that, it's not empty.

_____

What do you call a man who is shaking in a pile of leaves?

Russell.

Why are spiders so smart?

They can find everything they need to know on the web.

What do turkeys and teddy bears have in common?

They both have stuffing.

I sold glasses for a while, but I couldn't really see myself making any money.

_____

How many apples grow on a tree?

All of them!

I'm reading a book about anti-gravity...

... and I just can't put it down!

I was going to quit all my bad habits for the new year.

But then I remembered that nobody likes a quitter.

———————

Some people claim filling animals with helium is wrong.

I say, whatever floats your goat...

What do you call it when a group of apes starts a company?

Monkey business.

————————

How many telemarketers does it take to change a lightbulb?

Only one, but he has to do it during dinner.

What side of a turkey has the most feathers?

The outside!

———

I told my doctor I kept hearing this buzzing sound.

She said it's just a bug that's going around.

What happened when two pieces of bread went on a blind date?

It was loaf at first sight.

When you look for something, why is it always in the last place you look?

Because when you find it, you stop looking.

What does a baby computer call his father?

Data.

_____

Why couldn't Cleopatra accept Mark Antony's death?

She was the Queen of Denial.

Did you know that envelopes can't reproduce?

It's because they're all mail.

_____

How do you measure the quality of my puns?

A sighs-mograph.

Daughter: Is Mom making spaghetti for dinner?

Dad: I wouldn't put it pasta.

I just found out
Albert Einstein was
a real person.

I thought he was
just a theoretical
physicist.

How come you never see a train choke?

Because they always remember to choo.

———————

I bought a fresh loaf of bread today and it made my face pucker.

It's not bad, but it is a little sourdough.

I walked out of the barber's hating my haircut.

A few days later, it's started to grow on me.

———

When the water asked the sand if it could touch it, the sand said...

"Shore!"

What do you call a woman who is always sitting on the toilet?

Lou.

_____

I bought some French bread at the market.

They asked me, "Paper or plastic?"

I said, "Just baguette up."

How does a Spanish mushroom say
"please"?

Spore favor.

_____

They say talk is cheap...

... but have you ever talked to a lawyer?

Did you hear about the new AI company run by goats?

They're using bleating edge technology.

My stock in the ice-cream company took a dip.

_____

How can you tell which rabbits are the oldest in a group?

Just look for the grey hares.

Some people have trouble telling pastries and confections apart...

... but to me, it's a piece of cake.

On my way to work this morning, I saw some pallbearers carrying a coffin.

After work, I saw them again, carrying the same coffin.

I thought to myself, "Wow, these guys have lost the plot."

How would a satisfied poker dealer describe his job?

Ideal.

What do you call a woman who has one leg longer than the other?

Eileen.

_____

The workers who built the pyramids gave birth to a new profession as their backs buckled under pressure.

They had to go to the Cairo-practor.

I'm on a seafood diet.

Every time I see food, I eat it.

_____

What do you call a transformer that turns into a canoe?

A rowbot.

What do you get when you cross an airplane with an accountant?

A Boring 747.

How do you use a block of Cheddar cheese in a sword fight?

First, make sure it's extra sharp.

I went to buy some camouflage trousers yesterday, but I couldn't find any.

What is a physicist's favourite food?

Fission chips.

———

When the past, present and future go camping, they always argue.

It's intense, tenses in tents.

My ex-wife still misses me.

But her aim is starting to improve.

———————

How does an attorney sleep?

First, he lies on one side, then he lies on the other.

What do you call a
vampire duck?

Count Quackula.

Why are frogs so happy?

They eat whatever bugs them.

———————

The machine at the coin factory has suddenly stopped working, with no explanation.

It just doesn't make any cents.

What do you call a super-articulate dinosaur?

A thesaurus.

Why aren't dogs good dancers?

Because they have two left feet!

———

A doctor fell on his funny bone.

The nurse told him it was a
humerus incident.

What do you call a man who has cat scratches all over his face?

Claude.

_____

How do dentists practise?

They go through lots of drills.

When chemists die, they barium.

What brand of underwear do scientists wear?

Kelvin Klein.

Of all the inventions of the last 100 years, the dry erase board has to be the most remarkable.

What is a guitar player's favourite Italian food?

Strum-boli.

———

What do you call a wizard who's really bad at football?

Fumbledore.

I'm addicted to collecting vintage Beatles albums.

I need *Help!*

When I was a kid, my mother told me I could be anyone I wanted to be.

But it turns out identity theft is a crime.

———

What do you call a man who fixes potholes for a living?

Phil.

I poured some water over a duck's back yesterday.

He didn't seem to mind.

————————

What's green and has wheels?

Grass.

(I lied about the wheels.)

What do you call a man who has seagulls landing on the side of his head?

Cliff.

———

A buddy asked me how many salmon I caught.

I told him it's not polite to fish and tell.

I have a joke about trickle-down economics...

... but 99 per cent of you will never get it.

Interviewer: Thanks for applying for this job. First of all, where do you see yourself in five years?

Me: I think we'll still be using mirrors in five years.

My grief counsellor died the other day.

He was so good at his job, I don't even care.

———

Give a man a plane ticket and he flies for the day.

Push him out of the plane at 3,000 feet and he'll fly for the rest of his life.

What do you call bears with no ears?

B.

_____

Did you hear the latest trend is installing trampolines on cruise ships?

Now everyone is jumping on board.

What do you call a guy who
keeps vomiting?

Chuck.

_____

When I see the names of lovers
engraved on a tree, I don't find it cute
or romantic.

I find it weird how many people take
knives with them on dates.

After dinner last night, my wife asked if I could clear the table.

I needed a running start, but I made it.

I was sitting on the back porch with my husband when I suddenly blurted out, "I love you."

"Is that you or the beer talking?" he asked.

I answered, "It's me… talking to my beer."

———————

Marriage involves three rings: the engagement ring, the wedding ring and the suffer-ring.

My wife told me that I twist everything she says to my advantage.

I took that as a compliment.

———

My ex and I had a very amicable divorce.

I know this, because when I posted on Facebook, "I'm getting a divorce," he was the first one to like it.

My wife and I have decided not to have kids.

The kids are taking it pretty badly.

How does Satan like his pasta?

Al Dante.

When does a joke become a dad joke?

When it becomes apparent.

_____

I have a great joke about nepotism...

... but I'll only tell it to my kids.

What happened when the ten-year-old cannibal spilled his soup?

His mother gave him an earful.

Today, I visited my childhood home. I asked the residents if I could come in because I was feeling nostalgic. They slammed the door in my face.

My parents are the worst.

My parents raised
me as an only child.

It really annoyed my
younger brother.

Dad: Son, I have to tell you something. You're adopted.

Son: Wow. OK. I think I want to meet my biological parents.

Dad: We *are* your biological parents. Now pack up, the new ones will pick you up in 20 minutes.

What word in the English language is always spelled wrong?

Wrong.

_____

Humans are born with four kidneys.

When they grow up, two of them become adult knees.

When I was a little kid, I used to pray for a bicycle. Then, as I grew older, I learned that's not how prayer works.

So I stole a bike... and prayed for forgiveness.

What do you call a snail that isn't moving?

An escar-stay.

Be kind to dentists.

They have fillings too, you know.

@DadSaysJokes is a community-run dad jokes network on Instagram, Facebook and Twitter, with over six million followers, inspired by the daily jokes of author Kit Chilvers' dad, Andrew.

Every day, followers submit their jokes and the team picks their favourites – or Dad just drops in his own zinger!

Kit, a young social networking influencer, started his career at the tender age of 14, when he created his original platform, Football.Newz. He has since added another nine platforms, including @PubityPets and monster meme page @Pubity, which has over 32 million followers.

Also available:

 @DadSaysJokes

 @Dadsaysjokes

 @DadSaysJokes